Ahmad's Journey

Written by Kerrie Shanahan

Illustrated by Meredith Thomas

Flying Start
to Literacy®

Contents

Chapter 1
A sad story

"I saw a mother and baby orangutan in the village this morning," said Ahmad's dad.

Ahmad and his best friend Rani looked at each other in surprise. They were listening to their dads talking. They usually talked about their work on the palm oil plantation, not about orangutans in the village!

Every Friday night, Ahmad's family would gather with their neighbours for dinner. The children would play games together, and after dinner, Ahmad and Rani would relax and listen to their dads talk. The conversation had never captured their attention, until now.

"Wow! I love orangutans," said Rani, enthusiastically.

"I do, too," said Rani's dad. "I remember sharing our rainforest home with orangutans."

"You lived in the rainforest?" asked Ahmad.

"Yes," said Rani's dad. "When I was young, my family lived a traditional lifestyle and the rainforest was our home. But, as more and more of the rainforest was lost, our tribe had to move into the village. Now many of us work at the plantation that took our home."

"But what about the orangutans in the village?" Rani was impatient to find out more. "What were they doing there?"

"The mother was looking for food," replied Ahmad's dad. "She must be starving. She looked thin and weak. I think I startled her because she took off, into the rainforest."

"Orangutans coming into the village is a big problem," said Rani's dad sadly.

"What do you mean?" queried Rani.

"Well, parts of the rainforest were destroyed to make way for the plantation," continued Rani's dad. "The orangutans lost much of their home and now it's difficult for them to find food so they come to the village and eat the village crops."

"That's terrible!" Rani shook her head and frowned.

"I know," sighed Ahmad's dad. "And worse still, I heard one of the farmers say that if the orangutans keep destroying his crops, he would have to shoot them."

"That CAN'T happen!" Rani jumped to her feet. "We must help! Why don't we feed the orangutans?"

"That would make the problem worse, Rani," said her dad. "The orangutans would rely on people for food, and ultimately for survival. They would start coming into the village all the time and would eat more and more of the village crops."

"And that would make the farmers really angry!" added Ahmad's dad.

"Well, it's not fair!" Rani stormed out of the house.

* * * * *

Earlier that day, in the steamy, tropical rainforest next to Ahmad's village, the mother orangutan searched for food. Her new baby clung to her chest as she expertly swung through the lush trees that made up their home.

But this orangutan was feeling tired and weak. She had not been able to find enough food for her baby, or for herself. She needed to stay healthy and she needed to be able to make milk for her hungry, vulnerable baby.

The orangutan had seen the plants that grew in neat rows outside the safety of her rainforest home. She had also seen humans. The orangutan's instincts told her to be wary of humans; however, the need to feed her baby was stronger.

So, on that hot, sunny morning, the mother orangutan edged closer and closer to the delicious-looking plants. They were right there in front of her – easy to collect, easy to eat.

Just as she was about to venture towards the plants, a noise startled her. She sensed danger. She turned, scurried away and disappeared into the safety of the rainforest. Her heart was beating fast. The mother orangutan and her baby were safe for now, but she knew that soon she would need to try again.

Chapter 2
Rani's secret

"I have to save that orangutan and her baby," Rani told Ahmad. The determination in her voice made Ahmad take notice. "I'm going to the rainforest in the morning and I'll give them some fruit. That will stop them eating the farmers' crops."

"But you heard your dad!" Ahmad was shocked at Rani's suggestion. "It's not good for people to feed the orangutans."

"But it's not good for the orangutans to starve either!" insisted Rani. "I'm doing it! Will you come with me?"

Ahmad didn't answer straight away. He didn't want the orangutans to get hurt, but the thought of going into the rainforest sent a shiver down his spine.

"Um, I can't," he stammered. "I have to go to the market with Mum."

"Well, I'm going!" Rani had made up her mind. "But don't tell anyone," Rani demanded. "Promise?"

Ahmad hesitated. "Okay," he finally said. "I promise."

But he couldn't shake the sick feeling in the pit of his stomach.

On Monday morning, Ahmad and Rani walked to school together.

"I fed the orangutan and her baby on the weekend," said Rani proudly. "She was high up in a tree with her little baby clinging to her."

"Weren't you scared?" asked Ahmad. Just thinking about what Rani did made Ahmad's heart beat like a drum.

Rani looked at Ahmad oddly. "I wasn't scared at all! The mother looked me right in the eye. It was like she wanted to thank me."

"Orangutans are wild animals," warned Ahmad. "I wouldn't get too close if I were you."

Rani stopped and looked at Ahmad. A smile crept onto her face. "You're scared, Ahmad, aren't you? You're scared of going into the rainforest. You're scared of orangutans!"

"No, I'm not," said Ahmad, but he couldn't keep the quiver out of his voice.

"Well, come with me after school then," challenged Rani.

"I can't," said Ahmad hurriedly. "I have to look after my little sister."

Rani raised her eyebrows. She wasn't sure Ahmad was telling the truth, but she decided to let it go.

"Just make sure you don't tell anyone what I'm doing," she said firmly. "It's our secret."

"Sure," said Ahmad.

But, he wasn't sure at all. He wasn't sure about anything. But Rani was sure. He wished he could be brave and determined like she was. He wished he could do something important and worthwhile.

* * * * *

The orangutan mother and her baby were huddled together high in the canopy of the rainforest. Suddenly, the mother was on full alert. She heard a sound on the forest floor and tightened her grip on her baby.

Then the mother saw what had made the noise – a small human. The human was striding through the forest, looking up at the tops of the trees. The mother was about to flee when the human unexpectedly looked straight at her. The mother orangutan froze and met the human's gaze. The orangutan sensed that this human did not want to hurt her or her baby, but she was still on edge. She was ready to do anything to protect her baby.

The mother orangutan watched as the human placed something at the bottom of the tree. Then the human looked up and locked eyes with the mother orangutan again. After what seemed like forever, the small human finally turned and walked away.

The mother waited until she was sure the human had gone. Then, cautiously, she climbed to the bottom of the tree and examined what the human had left. Food! Delicious food! She scooped it up and scurried back to the safety of the canopy.

That day, the mother and baby ate well and that night they slept in their nest, feeling full and content.

Chapter 3

Rani goes missing

One afternoon after school, Rani's mother came rushing over to Ahmad's house.

"Ahmad!" she called frantically. "Have you seen Rani? She should be home by now."

"I haven't seen her." Ahmad's stomach did a flip.

"Rani's been coming home late every day this week." Rani's mother frowned, deep in thought. "I wonder what she's up to."

Ahmad knew that Rani was in the rainforest, but he had promised not to tell. His mind raced. What should he do? Rani's mother seemed very worried.

"I can go and look for Rani," he said eventually.

"Thank you, Ahmad." Rani's mother gave him a quick hug. She was relieved.

It was late in the afternoon when Ahmad reached the
edge of the thick, green rainforest. His heart was beating
fast and his stomach felt light and fluttery. He was
scared, very scared.

Ahmad's mind instantly flashed back to one of his earliest memories.

He was only four years old, but at the time he felt big and important because he was playing with his older cousins and their friends.

"Let's play hide-and-seek in the forest," suggested the biggest kid. The group cheered in agreement and marched with purpose towards the dark, dense forest.

The next thing Ahmad remembered was hiding by himself behind a vine-covered tree. He was still. And he was silent.

Suddenly, a huge orange-haired creature came from nowhere and scampered right past him, straight up the thick tree he was hugging.

"Ahhhh!" Ahmad ran. He'd never seen anything so frightening! He stumbled blindly through the forest, with tears streaming down his face. He ran into plants and tripped over the roots of massive trees. These images haunted him and he knew he was lucky the big kids had been there to rescue him.

Ahmad hadn't been back into the forest since that terrifying day. He shook his head and his thoughts returned to the present – to Rani, alone and scared in the forest.

"Come on, Ahmad," he said to himself. "It's just a forest. It's getting late and I must find Rani before it gets dark. Her mother is so worried."

Ahmad took a deep breath. He entered the forest where the tall trees and thick plants quickly engulfed him.

"Keep going." He urged himself forward. Even though he was scared, there was no turning back now.

Chapter 4

Brave Ahmad

"Rani?" called Ahmad as he walked deeper and deeper into the rainforest.

Suddenly, Ahmad heard a sound. It was the thrashing about of branches and it was coming from high up in the trees.

He looked up and saw an orangutan with a baby clinging to her. The orangutan was staring at him.

"Ahhh!" screamed Ahmad. He wanted to turn and run, but he was frozen with fear. His breathing was heavy and quick. He stood still, eyes wide with terror.

Time stood still. Ahmad didn't take his eyes off the orangutan. And the orangutan didn't take her eyes off Ahmad.

As Ahmad kept looking into the orangutan's large eyes, he slowly started to calm down. He realised that the orangutan looked kind, not threatening. He took a few uncertain steps towards her. The orangutan calmly moved to the next tree and then looked back at Ahmad.

I think she wants me to follow her, thought Ahmad.

He couldn't really believe this would be true, but what choice did he have? He had to trust the orangutan if he had any chance of finding Rani.

Ahmad followed the orangutan as she swung through the trees, but the rainforest was thick with vegetation and it was getting darker and darker. Ahmad struggled to keep sight of the orangutan.

And then she was gone.

"Oh no," panicked Ahmad. But bravely he kept running. He had to find Rani.

"Rani!" he called desperately. "Rani!"

There was no answer.

Then incredibly, Ahmad heard the orangutan again.
He looked up and there she was!

"She's come back for me." Relief flooded through
Ahmad's body.

The orangutan swung through the trees and Ahmad
followed her deeper into the thick rainforest. And then,
at last, Ahmad spotted Rani huddled on the ground.

"Rani!" cried Ahmad. He ran to her. "Are you okay?"

"I fell and hurt my ankle. I can't walk," sobbed Rani.
"How did you ever find me?"

"I had a bit of help," said Ahmad. "From your orangutan
friend."

Rani and Ahmad looked up. The orangutan and
her baby looked down at them from the top of a tall
rainforest tree.

"Now, let's get home," said Ahmad, as he helped Rani to
her feet. "It's almost nighttime."

* * * * *

The mother orangutan scanned the forest, looking for the small human that brought her food. The mother and her baby were getting used to this delicious food and it was about this time each day that she appeared.

The mother orangutan was pleased when she finally saw her. Like always, the orangutan watched as the human placed the food at the bottom of a tree and then waited for her to leave.

But this time was different. As the human turned to go, she tripped and fell. She let out a shrill scream! The human was hurt.

The mother orangutan watched protectively as the small human began to cry.

It was starting to get dark in the forest. A strange noise made the orangutan look away and into the thick forest. She heard the noise again and knew that it was another human. Although her instinct urged her to turn and flee from the human sound, something made her move towards it. She gathered her baby to her chest and quietly swung through the trees.

When the mother orangutan saw this "new" human, she knew that he was petrified, but she also sensed that he was there to help.

She wanted him to find the small human who brought her food so she swung through the trees, all the time looking back to encourage the frightened human to follow her.

He did follow!

The mother orangutan watched as the two humans saw each other and then left her forest together.

Chapter 5

A safe home

Rani's mother was relieved when she saw Ahmad and Rani stumble out of the rainforest, just as the stars in the night sky became visible.

"Rani! I'm so glad you're Okay!" Rani and her mother hugged tightly. "But look at your swollen ankle. We had better get you to the hospital."

At the hospital, a doctor examined Rani's ankle.

"It's a bad sprain," the doctor explained. "You won't be able to walk on it for a while, but it will heal in a few weeks."

"Thank you, doctor," said Rani's mother. "If Ahmad hadn't found Rani in the forest, I dread to think about what might have happened."

"What were you doing in the forest?" asked the doctor.

Rani explained how she had been feeding the orangutan and her baby.

"I thought I was helping," Rani concluded miserably. "But I just made things worse. The orangutans still don't have enough food and I don't know what will happen to them."

"Maybe I can help." The doctor handed Rani a card. "I have a friend who works at an orangutan rescue centre. They relocate orangutans who have lost their homes or don't have enough food."

"That's exactly what we need," said Rani excitedly.

The next morning, Rani and her mother called the number on the card. They explained what had happened.

"Can you show us approximately where the orangutan's home range is?" the rescue worker asked Rani.

"I won't be able to show you because I've hurt my ankle," replied Rani. "But I know somebody who can."

The next week, some workers from the orangutan rescue centre met Rani and Ahmad at the edge of the rainforest. Rani outlined the general area where the orangutan and her baby lived in the forest.

"Great," said one of the workers. "We will find the orangutan and her baby, tranquillise them and relocate them. We know an area of forest where there is plenty of food. They will be safe and happy in their new home."

"Thank you," said Rani. "Ahmad can show you which way to go."

"Sure." Ahmad nodded confidently. "Follow me!"

Rani smiled as she watched Ahmad, her loyal and sensible friend, lead the rescue workers into the forest.

* * * * *

The mother orangutan was feeling particularly weak. The small human had not brought any food for some time and she no longer had the energy to search too widely for food in the forest.

The mother instinctively clutched her baby tightly to her chest as she noticed a group of humans walking straight towards them. The humans surrounded their tree. Her baby was frightened, and so was she.

She looked around desperately for a way to escape, but before she could move, a sudden, sharp pain shot through her thigh. Her world spun, and then nothing.

* * * * *

Months later, the mother orangutan and her baby were swinging happily through the trees in their new rainforest home. Their new home had an abundant supply of diverse fruits for the orangutans to feed on. The mother was feeling strong and energetic and her baby was healthy and growing rapidly. Being tranquillised and moved by the group of humans was now only a dim memory for the mother and her baby.

The mother orangutan had another faint memory – a memory of two small humans who had been kind and friendly and brave.

A note from the author

Whenever I visit our city zoo, I love watching the orangutans as they swing, climb, play and eat. And it appears that the orangutans love watching us, too. Their eyes are full of curiosity as they study the people who are studying them! It has made me wonder just who is watching who and what they might be thinking about us. This thought was in my mind as I was coming up with ideas for my story.

I grew up near a forest in Australia. My brothers and I often explored the forest when we were children. This made me wonder what it must be like for children growing up near rainforests. Do they like to explore the forest? Do they ever catch glimpses of orangutans? And, if they do, are they scared of them? Or are they drawn to them?

As I thought about these questions, the characters of Ahmad and Rani began to develop in my mind. And so the story of how Ahmad overcame his fear to help the orangutans was born.